Is Rob Fit?

Written by
Stephen Rickard

Illustrated by
Ruth Bennett

Tess is fit.

Tess can run.

Pip is fit.

Pip can run.

Rob is not fit.
Rob can not run.

Rob can get fit.

Rob can huff and puff.

Is Rob fit?

Get set. Go!

Go, Rob, go!

Rob is as fit as Tess and Pip.